ethics
activities

bju **press**®

Greenville, South Carolina

Note: The fact that materials produced by other publishers may be referred to in this volume does not constitute an endorsement of the content or theological position of materials produced by such publishers. Any references and ancillary materials are listed as an aid to the student or the teacher and in an attempt to maintain the accepted academic standards of the publishing industry.

ETHICS Student Activities

Writers
Kevin Collins, MDiv
Paul Hornor, MDiv
Bruce Ostrom, PhD

Writer Consultants
Tom Parr, ThM
L. Michelle Rosier

Biblical Worldview
Brian C. Collins, PhD

Academic Integrity
Jeff Heath, EdD

Instructional Design
Rachel Santopietro, MEd
Michael Winningham, MA

Editor
James Zemke, MA

Book Concept and Design
Alayna Rowan

Cover Designer
Emily Rush

Illustrators
Jon Andrews
Jullianna Echardt
Roy Hermelin (Beehive Illustration)
Augusto Zambonato

Production Designer
Sherry McCollough

Permissions
Maria Andersen
Ruth Bartholomew
Sylvia Gass
Hannah Labadorf
Jennifer Walton

Project Coordinators
Allison Brooks
Heather Chisholm

Postproduction Liaison
Peggy Hargis

Photo Credits
Cover Pyrosky/E+ via Getty Images; **39** SDI Productions/E+ via Getty Images; **49** cirano83/iStock/ Getty Images Plus via Getty Images; **55** Ground Picture/Shutterstock.com; **59** 3D_generator/iStock/ Getty Images Plus via Getty Images; **67** michaeljung/Shutterstock.com; **71** fizkes/Shutterstock.com; **77** georgeclerk/E+ via Getty Images

Text acknowledgments appear on-page with text selections.

The text for this book is set in Adobe Minion Pro, Adobe Myriad Pro, Calibri by Monotype, DIN 2014 by Paratype, Free 3 of 9 by Matthew Welch, Freight Macro by Joshua Darden, Freight Sans by Joshua Darden, and Times New Roman PSMT.

contents

using the activities

As you engage with the issues surrounding ethics, you will develop greater aptitude for handling difficult situations with more practice. These activities provide opportunities to practice what you're learning. Many of the activities you do and the skills you hone will be valuable not only for this course but also for life.

ACTIVITIES

The activities will guide you as you engage with each topic. A variety of instructions and questions will help you learn how to carefully apply a Christian ethic.

PRAYER JOURNAL

The prayer journal will help you pray specifically and scripturally based on each lesson's theme.

SCRIPTURE MEMORY

Scripture memory presents key verses related to the lessons. Each Scripture passage includes a brief explanation of the passage's significance.

1.1 God's Character Is the Starting Point

We can search all over the world for a basis for good and moral living. Throughout history, people have chosen to ground their ethics in the stars, mythological gods, or human reason, among other fallible and finite foundations. Only God is eternal, infinite, omnipotent, omniscient, and omnipresent. God's character is perfect and unchanging and, therefore, is a fundamental foundation for ethics.

THE ATTRIBUTES OF GOD AS A BASIS FOR ETHICS

Choose one of the attributes of God discussed in the Student Edition (holiness, love, goodness, righteousness, trustworthiness) and summarize it below. Explain why it is a key character trait for Christian ethics.

_____

_____

_____

_____

Choose one of the following attributes of God not covered in the Student Edition and explain how it impacts Christian ethics.

Truthfulness: _____

_____

_____

Graciousness/mercifulness: _____

_____

_____

_____

_____

Faithfulness: _____

_____

_____

_____

1.2 Creational Norms and Two Genders

The unbelieving world will fight against God and the order He has established in the universe He created. The fact that God created two genders is seen in Genesis 1–2 and then throughout all of Scripture as well as throughout the created order. Because of this, the creational norm for human genders is that there are just two genders, man and woman.

CREATIONAL NORMS APPLIED TO HUMAN SEXUALITY AND GENDER

Read the article "He Made Them Male and Female: Sex, Gender, and the Image of God" by Christopher Yuan. Describe how the unbelieving world pushes back against God's creational order by trying to establish a new norm for their corrupted views on sexuality and gender.

_____

_____

_____

_____

_____

In your own words, describe the biblical and Christian position of the creational norm regarding human sexuality and gender.

_____

_____

_____

_____

_____

_____

_____

_____

_____

Making ethical choices can be difficult because of the fallenness of our own hearts, the fallenness of the culture around us, and the fallenness of a world affected by a curse.

Identify an ethical difficulty in each of the following three categories. Relate how the effects of the Fall in each category make ethical decision-making difficult.

THE FALLENNESS OF OUR OWN HEARTS

_____

_____

_____

_____

_____

_____

_____

_____

THE FALLENNESS OF THE CULTURE

_____

_____

_____

_____

_____

_____

THE EFFECTS OF A SIN-CURSED WORLD

_____

_____

_____

_____

_____

_____

_____

_____

Read the following scenarios and identify the approach with one of the following options. Explain your answer.

Deontological Ethics

CONSEQUETIALIST ETHICS
Utilitarian Ethics
Situation Ethics
Ethical Egoism

Virtue Ethics

Existentialism

SCENARIO 1

A health care system is considering allocating the nation's limited medical resources based on a citizen's ability to contribute to the overall welfare of the nation. Providing health care for an individual with no possibility of recovering deprives other citizens of medical attention, and therefore, is not good policy for the majority of citizens. The issue here is not the rationing of limited resources, which would be necessary under any medical system, but the fact that given the limited resources, individuals should be treated based on their ability to contribute to society.

_____

_____

_____

_____

SCENARIO 2

A relative implores you and your family to demonstrate love by happily attending another relative's same-sex wedding ceremony. Many in your family would regard it offensive and unloving if you decided not to attend. The relative argues that a Christian should attend the wedding to show his love for his family member and that his attendance does not equal support for same-sex relationships.

_____

_____

SCENARIO 3

A guy breaks off a dating relationship because he is not sure he's dating for the right reasons. He is concerned that he is dating just to satisfy some selfish desire for happiness. He says he wants a relationship where he can offer disinterested loyalty without seeking any benefit from the relationship.

_____

_____

_____

_____

SCENARIO 4

A friend counsels you with this advice: "It's your life. Don't let your parents get in the way of you fulfilling your dreams." You decide to dismiss your parents' concerns about your relationships and choice of college because you are determined to find a partner who makes you happy and attend a college that prepares you for a financially successful career. You plan to do what suits your own desires and plans.

_____

_____

_____

_____

SCENARIO 5

You've grown up in a fairly sheltered home which followed several traditional social expectations. But now that you have left and are at college, your roommate is opening up a whole new world of possibilities to you—possibilities that were not encouraged or even talked about back home. "You can be anything you want to be! Don't let social conventions hinder you by forcing you into an inferior role. Reject the status quo. Embrace self-care and self-empowerment. Love yourself and be your own greatest hero."

_____

_____

_____

SCENARIO 6

Your classmate is making unintentional mistakes on a project that the two of you are working on together. You need to confront her about these mistakes, but you are nervous about offending her. You decide to begin with a word of appreciation for her help on the project. You then gently point out the areas in the project that need correction by recommending a solution.

_____

_____

_____

2.3 Critiquing the Ethical Approaches

Re-read the scenarios from Activity 2.2 and provide a one- to two-paragraph critique of each one.

SCENARIO 1

_____

_____

_____

_____

_____

_____

_____

_____

_____

SCENARIO 1

_____

_____

_____

_____

_____

_____

_____

_____

SCENARIO 3

_____

_____

_____

_____

_____

_____

_____

_____

SCENARIO 4

_____

_____

_____

_____

_____

_____

_____

_____

_____

SCENARIO 5

_____

_____

_____

_____

_____

_____

_____

SCENARIO 6

_____

_____

_____

_____

_____

_____

_____

3.1 Delighting in God's Law

You have learned of the necessity of an objective moral standard for discerning right from wrong. It is one thing to be convinced that God's law is the standard for human behavior; it is another thing to delight in God's law. In reaction to secular society's rejection of biblical morality as outlined in the Ten Commandments, some Christians might misuse the Mosaic law, treating it as an abstract code of ethics for curbing the moral decline of society. But this is not the same as producing changed hearts. For society to conform to God's law, people need to delight in it from the heart. This activity is intended to help you delight in God's law.

Answer the following questions for the purpose of (1) evaluating your own heart attitude toward God's law and (2) applying the principles of this lesson to influence others to have the right attitude toward God's law.

1. **Even Christians struggle to delight in God's law as they should. Can you think of some reasons for your own struggle in this area?**

_____

_____

_____

_____

_____

_____

2. **How might an understanding of God's law as a reflection of God's character increase your delight in His law?**

_____

_____

_____

_____

_____

_____

3. How would you respond to someone who tells you he does not concern himself with the Ten Commandments, but he insists that his ethics leads him to do the loving thing in every situation?

_____

_____

_____

4. Someone tells you that society is morally bankrupt because it has rejected God's law. She argues that the moral condition of people would improve if the government enforced the Mosaic law. How would you respond to this person?

_____

_____

_____

_____

_____

5. What is the relationship between the Ten Commandments and creational norms? How might an understanding of this relationship help you better delight in God' law?

_____

_____

_____

_____

_____

6. Since Christ has fulfilled the Mosaic law on behalf of all who trust Him, what value does the Mosaic law have for Christians?

_____

_____

_____

7. Do you think you would delight in God's law apart from the New Covenant promise of the Holy Spirit? Why?

_____

_____

_____

_____

_____

8. Why is it impossible for a person with the Spirit to be indifferent to God's law?

_____

_____

9. How would you respond to someone who tells you that Christians are not obligated to keep the law because they are no longer under the law?

_____

_____

_____

10. The grammar of the gospel teaches us that the *imperatives* (what we must do as Christians) are made possible because of the *indicatives* (what Christ has done for us). How do you think you would respond to the ethical demands of God's law if Christ had not freed you from its condemnation?

_____

_____

_____

11. Christians are called to imitate Christ in holy living, but how can they do this without turning imitation into a self-help strategy for ethical living?

_____

_____

_____

12. What would you say to a fellow Christian who sees his identity strictly in terms of his failures?

_____

_____

_____

3.2 Growing in Wisdom

You've learned about the close relationship between wisdom and law and the fact that both are based on creational norms. Becoming a Christian does not automatically make a person wise. To navigate life in this fallen world, believers need to grow in discernment, prudence, and virtue. Recall that wisdom is defined as the art of living well by observing creational norms through the lens of Scripture, by listening to the counsel of the wise, and by being conscious that all of life is lived before the face of God. This activity is intended to help you evaluate competing theories of ethical living based on biblical wisdom as presented in section 3.2.

Read the article "Four Ways to Live More Ethically" by Thomas G. Plante.

1. Summarize the main points of the article.

_____

_____

_____

_____

_____

_____

2. Identify one strength and one weakness of each point from the article based on biblical wisdom as presented in section 3.2.

_____

_____

_____

_____

_____

_____

You have learned about the role of motives in making ethical decisions. Why we do is just as important as what we do. In the Christian understanding of ethics, doing the right thing for the wrong reasons does not make an action ethical. A Christian's action is ethical when motived by a desire for God to be glorified in the action. This is the teleology of Christian ethics. While Christians may have additional motives behind their actions, their choices in life should show that God is their greatest delight. This activity is intended to help you live for God's glory.

Answer the following questions to help you evaluate the motives behind your choices and formulate a plan to make God's glory the ultimate motive in your life.

1. As you think back on a recent ethical decision in your life, what were your motives behind the decision you made?

   _____

   _____

2. What questions might you ask yourself to evaluate whether your decision in a particular situation is rightly motivated?

   _____

   _____

   _____

3. A businesswoman tells you that she financially supports several charitable organizations because it makes her business more profitable. What is your assessment of this person's charitable giving?

   _____

   _____

4. How can delighting in God help you perform a difficult or undesirable duty?

   _____

   _____

   _____

5. A person chooses to suffer for the sake of Christ rather than enjoy the fleeting pleasures of sin for a season. How does this choice glorify God?

   _____

   _____

6. Living out the Christian ethic in this fallen world can be difficult because the things in this world can be deceptively attractive. How can the values of the kingdom of God help you remain faithful to God when tempted to compromise?

_____

_____

_____

7. Jesus motivated His disciples to ethical living by teaching about the amazing blessings that awaited them in the world to come. Do these things motivate you to ethical living? Why?

_____

_____

8. Someone tells you that he thinks Jesus' promise about the meek inheriting the earth is nonsense. His life experience has taught him that those who succeed in this world are the ones who are willing to make ethical compromises. How would you respond to this person?

_____

_____

_____

_____

9. Jesus promised that the pure in heart will see God. How might this beatitude defend against sexual lust?

_____

_____

_____

_____

10. How can God's promise of a glorious future with Him strengthen your resolve as a Christian to live for His glory in this present evil age?

_____

_____

_____

Choose one of the virtues listed on the chart below (found on page 65 of your textbook). Complete a Bible study of that virtue, particularly focused on the Wisdom Books in the Bible. Create a presentation on the virtue and what the Bible says about the virtue: definition, description, cultivation and development, and application of the virtue. Your presentation may be a paper, a slide presentation, a blog post, a pamphlet, or other creative idea.

VIRTUES
faith
love
hope
righteousness
goodness
prudence
diligence
faithfulness
courage
self-control
temperance
patience
humility
meekness
gentleness
kindness
compassion
gratitude
joy
peace
honesty

4.2 Practicing the Spiritual Disciplines

Choose one of the following spiritual disciplines: Bible study, prayer, local church participation, putting sin to death. Request book suggestions from pastors, parents, teachers, or other spiritual mentors on the topic of the spiritual discipline you chose. Read the book (or applicable sections of a book) on that topic. Outline practical ways you can make the spiritual discipline a part of the fabric of your life.

_____

_____

_____

_____

_____

_____

_____

_____

_____

_____

_____

_____

_____

_____

Being an ethical person consists of soul-rooted realities, without which it is impossible to manifest the Christian ethic in real-life situations. The virtue of faith is one of these soul-rooted realities. Like an iceberg, the largest chunk of our ethical nature lies beneath the surface of our lives. Therefore, it is vital that we examine ourselves to ascertain the condition of our soul.

Read the following scenarios to assist in your self-examination. Choose two of the four scenarios and write your response.

SCENARIO ONE

Julie is a professing Christian who is very knowledgeable about the Bible, and she serves diligently in her church. She attends all the weekly meetings and is highly respected for her tireless efforts in writing cards to elderly members, working in the nursery, and teaching a women's Bible study. Other church members speak of her as a model Christian, which Julie very much enjoys hearing. She finds her worth and significance in the validation of others rather than in knowing Christ, and she prides herself in her knowledge and service rather than glorifying God for what He has done. Julie is often impatient and critical of other church members who lack her zeal and discipline. She thinks people should be more like her and try harder to be better Christians.

_____

_____

_____

_____

_____

_____

SCENARIO TWO

Bobby is known at school for his self-confidence, approaching every aspect of life according to the motto "If it's going to be, it's up to me." His self-confidence has grown over the years as his academic success has validated his perception of himself as intellectually superior to others. On the football field, Bobby has distinguished himself as the strongest and fastest athlete on the team. Bobby does not worry about facing challenges too great for him. He is convinced he has the capacity to handle whatever life presents. He regards faith in God as a crutch for weak people who are not strong enough to stand on their own two feet.

_____

_____

_____

_____

_____

SCENARIO THREE

Trent considers himself a very spiritual Christian, but he views doctrinal formulations of Christianity to be lifeless and boring. While Trent says that he respects the Bible, he doesn't think knowledge of the Bible is necessary for a robust life of faith. "Reason," he says, "is at odds with faith because faith is like jumping into the unknown." Trent is convinced that his faith is virtuous because it is not limited to what the Bible teaches. He thinks that openness to various spiritual concepts and a preference for ambiguities about the supernatural produces the best kind of ethical behavior.

_____

_____

_____

_____

_____

_____

_____

SCENARIO FOUR

Sarah is a quiet and unassuming young lady who displays genuine kindness to others. Although her life is filled with difficult and trying circumstances, she exudes a warmth and joy that others attribute to her love for Christ. Sarah is not able to engage in a lot of church activities because of her health problems, but she enjoys reading God's Word and sharing with her friends what God is teaching her. She always seems to be humble in how she discusses the Bible. Because she is aware of the pull of her sinful flesh, Sarah daily depends on the Lord to live an ethical life. Her Christlikeness is evident to all. She trusts that God loves her and that He knows what is best for her life. Therefore, she bases her ethical decisions on the promises of God rather than what she can see with her eyes.

_____

_____

_____

_____

_____

_____

_____

5.2 Evaluating Definitions of Love

You've learned about the direct connection between the things we love and our ethical choices. To be virtuous, we must love that which is good and true as defined by Scripture. What makes love virtuous is not the word itself; many people frequently abuse the word "love" by using vague and empty terms to define it. Evaluate the following video based on a biblical view of love.

Watch the video "5 Definitions of Love" by OWN (Oprah Winfrey Network).

1. Summarize the five definitions of love in the video.

_____

_____

_____

_____

_____

_____

_____

2. Evaluate each definition based on a biblical view of love.

_____

_____

_____

_____

_____

_____

_____

_____

_____

_____

_____

_____

_____

OWN. "5 Definitions of Love | SuperSoul Sunday | Oprah Winfrey Network." YouTube video, 2:25. Posted February 13. 2018. https://www.youtube.com/watch?v=qRjTZEkDm18.

5.3 Becoming a More Hopeful Person

You've learned about the necessity of having a well-founded hope. Given the hopelessness in the world today and the various ways that people vainly try to create hope apart from a biblical view of reality, it is essential that Christians nurture their hope in Christ.

The following biblical passages will assist you in your plan for becoming a more hopeful person. Commit to spending a few minutes each day meditating on them.

- Psalm 31:24: "Be of good courage, and he shall strengthen your heart, all ye that hope in the LORD."
- Psalm 42:11: "Why art thou cast down, O my soul? and why art thou disquieted within me? hope thou in God: for I shall yet praise him, who is the health of my countenance, and my God.
- Psalm 119:114: "Thou art my hiding place and my shield: I hope in thy word."
- Psalm 119:116: "Uphold me according unto thy word, that I may live: and let me not be ashamed of my hope."
- Jeremiah 17:7: "Blessed is the man that trusteth in the LORD, and whose hope the LORD is.
- Lamentations 3:24: "The LORD is my portion, saith my soul; therefore will I hope in him."
- Romans 5:3–5: "And not only so, but we glory in tribulations also: knowing that tribulation worketh patience; And patience, experience; and experience, hope: And hope maketh not ashamed; because the love of God is shed abroad in our hearts by the Holy Ghost which is given unto us."
- Romans 8:25: "But if we hope for that we see not, then do we with patience wait for it."
- Romans 15:13: "Now the God of hope fill you with all joy and peace in believing, that ye may abound in hope, through the power of the Holy Ghost."
- 1 Peter 1:3: "Blessed be the God and Father of our Lord Jesus Christ, which according to his abundant mercy hath begotten us again unto a lively hope by the resurrection of Jesus Christ from the dead."

6.1 The Essence of Virtue

While some unbelievers may display outward virtue, they are not what Scripture would call virtuous people. Their virtue is more like the artificial fruit some people showcase on their coffee table. Virtuous people, however, possess genuine spiritual fruit. The former may *display* aspects of virtue, whereas the latter *practice* the essence of virtue.

Answer the following questions to develop this topic.

1. **Based on your understanding of Galatians 5:22–23, do you believe unbelievers can truly possess and practice the virtues listed? Why?**

   _____

   _____

   _____

   _____

2. **According to Colossians 1:9–10, why can believers bear spiritual fruit and please the Lord with their lives?**

   _____

   _____

   _____

   _____

3. **According to 2 Peter 1:3–7, 10, how can people practice these virtues?**

   _____

4. **What key phrases from Ephesians 2:10 and Galatians 2:20 undergird the essence of virtue for believers?**

   _____

5. **The essence of virtue is** _____.

   A trying one's hardest

   B avoiding the vices

   C a God-centered approach to practicing the virtues

   D focusing primarily on faith, hope, and love

Any display of virtue by unbelievers doesn't change the fact that they have wrong sources, motives, methods, definitions, and applications of the virtues. Even when they borrow virtues from God's Word and display aspects of virtuous living, unbelievers still lack a holistic God-centered approach to practicing truly virtuous and ethical living.

CLARIFYING TERMS

Write the term that matches the appropriate scenario: "smart," "wise," or "prudent."

_____ **1.** Susie always packs a raincoat and an extra change of clothes when she goes hiking with her friends. It often rains spontaneously, making the trails muddy and slippery.

_____ **2.** Johnny chose the correct answer to the multiple-choice question because he understood the material and figured out the answer accordingly.

_____ **3.** Dave avoided violence in a fight that broke out at school by tactfully and firmly addressing each party's misunderstandings head-on.

THE APPLICATION TO ABORTION

Prudence is much more than a combination of the appropriate use of knowledge and well-timed wisdom. Consider the topic of abortion. The truth of Scripture is that murder is evil and sinful (Exod. 20:13; 1 Tim. 1:9). Therefore, the murder of any person (unborn, newborn, child, adult, or elderly) is the evil and sinful destruction of an image-bearer of God (Gen. 1:26–27; 9:6).

While pro-life advocates long for the day when abortion is outlawed, different approaches to this goal exist, and success might not guarantee the end of its practice. Some advocates focus primarily on incremental changes in abortion laws, seeking to gain as many limitations on abortion as possible—with the ultimate aim of prohibiting all abortions. Others argue that any law that does not immediately abolish all abortions is an unbiblical compromise. They call for laws to mandate the immediate abolition of abortion.

How might the virtue of prudence guide a Christian with respect to these two approaches to ending abortion?

_____

_____

_____

_____

The Place for Diligence, Faithfulness, and Courage

Look up and read each passage and summarize its teaching. Then answer the personal application question for each virtue.

Diligence: Colossians 3:17, 23

_____

_____

_____

_____

_____

What is one area of your life where you need greater diligence?

_____

Faithfulness: Philippians 3:12–21

_____

_____

_____

What is one area of your life which you are struggling to prioritize and be faithful to?

_____

Courage: Ephesians 6:10–20

_____

_____

_____

_____

_____

_____

_____

_____

_____

What is one area of your life where you habitually lack courage?

_____

List some first steps for developing a plan to practice diligence, faithfulness, and courage joyfully and intentionally.

_____

_____

_____

_____

_____

_____

_____

_____

According to the nuance brought out in defining self-control and temperance as we have done in this textbook, the following exercise will help solidify that nuance in practical ways.

Write *A* if the scenario demonstrates self-control or *B* if it demonstrates temperance.

_____ 1. When you and your friends go to a fast-food restaurant, even though they order burgers and fries and you want junk food, you order a salad instead.

_____ 2. Your friends invite you to go to the mall. Because you've been deliberately using God's Word to strengthen yourself against lust and prepare yourself for temptation, and because you have been virtuous in several recent incidental encounters with lust, you decide to go with them and commit yourself to remain strong against any struggles you might face.

_____ 3. You have seen the ways that you and others are easily distracted by social media, so you limit yourself to only one social media account and set up a plan to use it responsibly.

_____ 4. Your coach praises you for your hard work in practice and great performances in games. To avoid asserting yourself over your teammates and to avoid bragging, you choose to not let the coach's praise go to your head.

_____ 5. Your sibling accidentally ruins one of your favorite outfits. Rather than berating him or her and holding this against your sibling, you recognize how regretful your sibling is and decide to treat him or her with kindness.

_____ 6. Three months ago, you decided to give up soft drinks. While you struggled with the adjustment initially, today you choose to drink water or juice at restaurants and parties because you now genuinely prefer them to soda.

_____ 7. While you are on your phone, an ad with inappropriate content starts playing. You immediately block the ad and do what you can to prevent such material from reappearing in the app or browser.

_____ 8. You have read books and articles on humility and gratitude as a devotional practice. You recognize that pride can easily sneak up on you, and you know what it is like to indulge in and entertain pride. You decide to appreciate humility and gratitude, you enjoy seeing it in others, and you avoid speaking or acting in proud ways.

Imagine a scenario where you lack self-control and therefore struggle to say no to a particular sin. Write a proposal for how you can grow in this virtue.

_____

_____

_____

_____

_____

Imagine a scenario where you need to improve in temperance. Write a proposal for how you can grow in this virtue.

_____

_____

_____

_____

_____

Match the correct virtue/vice combination with its corresponding scenario.

> A humility/pride   B meekness/anger   C gentleness/harshness

_____ **1.** You disagree on various political points and minor issues of theology with certain friends and family members. You are entirely convinced of your positions. You are concerned about their views, which you see as wrong and unhelpful. You love them dearly, but your passion for defending the truth of your beliefs often gets the best of you.

_____ **2.** Your youth group at church spends time discussing frustrating topics about culture. You find them pointless, a waste of time, and repetitive; you also can't seem to pull your friends out of those discussions while being nice to them. You struggle to keep your cool and not snap at them.

_____ **3.** You believe that sharing pure facts is an honest and honorable way of reporting information—even if that information is all about you and your successes. You work hard and nothing you have achieved has been given to you. Your home life is challenging, and your parents are by no means wealthy. You crave the satisfaction you feel from sharing your accomplishments or ambitious plans with others.

Discuss in groups or list how each of the scenarios above affects your ethical decision-making regarding that specific virtue.

SCENARIO 1

_____

_____

_____

_____

SCENARIO 2

_____

_____

_____

_____

_____

_____

_____

SCENARIO 3

_____

_____

_____

_____

_____

_____

THE BIBLICAL MODEL OF HELPING THOSE WE CAN

Read the parable of the good Samaritan in Luke 10:25–37. With this biblical account and its teaching on true kindness and compassion in mind, answer the following questions.

1. What was the same in each case when the three men passed by the wounded Jew?

   _____

   _____

   _____

   _____

2. What other two related virtues (aside from kindness and compassion) are featured in this story?

   _____

3. Why did the Samaritan show kindness to and have compassion on the wounded Jew?

   _____

   _____

   _____

   _____

4. Who are your neighbors that God calls you to love?

   _____

5. Describe a circumstance where you would show kindness to someone with whom you normally wouldn't interact.

   _____

   _____

   _____

   _____

   _____

   _____

   _____

6. **Describe a circumstance where you would show compassion to someone with whom you normally wouldn't interact.**

_____

_____

_____

_____

_____

_____

A MODERN-DAY LESSON IN HELPING THOSE WE CAN

The situation in the Xinjiang region of China is dire. For many decades the Chinese minorities who live there, especially the Muslim Uyghurs, have suffered persecution from the Chinese government, and since 2016 the genocidal program against the Uyghur people has only gotten worse. What is threatened is the Uyghur identity, culture, language, dress, religion, health, freedom, and lives. Han Chinese, the majority people group in China, are being sent to Xinjiang to forcibly live with Uyghur families to keep tabs on them and be a Chinese majority influence on them. At least one million Uyghurs have been imprisoned for various "crimes" against the state. Forced sterilizations of women and forced labor are also common. In recent years, China has accelerated its once gradual mission to force the Uyghur people to assimilate into main Chinese culture and, sadly, that mission includes genocide. While the Chinese government denies all allegations, these are real crimes against humanity occurring in our day.

Listen to Part 3 of the January 19, 2022 episode of _The Briefing_ by Al Mohler (starting at 14:47) and evaluate the ethics of the situation.

There is no need to feel guilty about not being able to help those whom you can't help. You might desire to help a people group or an individual suffering persecution, but you don't have access to them. That is good and righteous. But because you have limitations, you can't do all that you might want to do to show compassion to hurting people. However, there are those who can do something and should.

1. **Given the situation of the Uyghur people and the comments made by Chamath Palihapitiya, what ethical choices are facing the NBA?**

_____

_____

_____

_____

2. How has Chamath Palihapitiya made an unethical choice?

_____

_____

_____

_____

3. What ethical approach are the NBA and Chamath Palihapitiya subscribing to by ignoring the plight of the Uyghur people and failing to show them kindness and compassion?

_____

4. How should kindness and compassion shape the responses of each person involved in the situation?

_____

_____

_____

_____

_____

_____

5. What ethical choices face fans of the Golden State Warriors or of the NBA?

_____

_____

_____

_____

_____

_____

6. Even though you aren't able to influence China to stop persecuting the Uyghur people, you can apply these principles to exercising kindness and compassion in your community. What ways could you endeavor to apply these principles by showing kindness and compassion in your community?

_____

_____

_____

_____

_____

_____

7.3 The Vice of Worry

Answer the following questions.

1. What sort of behavior results from excessive worrying?

   _____

   _____

2. What excuses are commonly given to justify excessive worrying?

   _____

   _____

The vice of worrying is related to anxiety, which is made up of uneasiness and fear. Believers should not be characterized by worry or anxiety. Peace is the virtue that the Spirit develops in the lives of believers, and that peace snuffs out worry.

Read 2 Corinthians 4:7–16. Answer the following questions based on this passage.

1. What virtues are referenced either explicitly or implicitly in this text?

   7: _____

   8: _____

   9: _____

   13: _____

   14: _____

   15: _____

   16: _____

2. Does this passage leave any room for the vice of worry to be part of a Christian's practice? Explain your answer.

   _____

   _____

   _____

3. What challenges are you facing today where you find yourself tempted to give in to the vice of worry rather than to the virtue of peace?

   _____

   _____

Describe how practicing the virtue of peace enables you to ethically manage the following situations.

SCENARIO ONE

A good friend has expressed serious doubts about her faith in the Bible as God's Word and in Jesus as a sufficient Savior.

_____

_____

_____

_____

SCENARIO TWO

Someone in your immediate family has received a life-threatening diagnosis.

_____

_____

_____

SCENARIO THREE

You are anxious about finishing high school with good grades, taking college entry exams, and getting into the college you want.

_____

_____

_____

_____

SCENARIO FOUR

Your friend group is going through some changes as people start dating or finding other interests.

_____

_____

_____

_____

7.4 Don't Tell Yourself Lies

Did you realize that the virtue of honesty includes telling yourself truths rather than lies?

To believe a lie is to tell yourself an untruth, which is harmful to your thinking, decision-making, and living. The pursuit of honesty includes not only speaking the truth and being honest in all your dealings but also guarding against telling yourself lies.

Use the following questions to create a personal environment that is hospitable to the virtue of honesty and inhospitable to the vices of lying and falsehood, even when you entertain them in your mind and embrace them in your heart.

1. What are some common lies that people your age are likely to believe?

_____

_____

_____

2. How would you correct these lies with the truth?

_____

_____

_____

_____

_____

_____

_____

_____

_____

_____

_____

_____

_____

_____

Write a paragraph explaining how believing a specific lie has harmed you. Include how understanding the biblical correction will benefit you moving forward.

_____

_____

_____

_____

_____

_____

_____

_____

_____

_____

_____

8.1 The Components for Making Ethical Decisions

Create a pamphlet, blog, slideshow, or other form of presentation that overviews Acts, Agents, Ends, and Context. Use that tool to present this information to someone outside your class. Ask that person or group to respond to the following questions.

1. List three insights into this biblical approach to ethics that you found helpful.

2. Identify two effects that you think this approach would have if more people followed it.

3. What is one question that you still have about this approach?

8.2 Using an Ethical Method: Test Cases

Choose two of the following topics. Write a test case for each of them regarding a hypothetical scenario that requires an ethical response. Discuss your test cases with a classmate or with the entire class. Be prepared to rightly answer the four main questions from the practical method for ethical decision-making.

Topics

- Abortion
- Addictive substances or habits (like gambling)
- Civil disobedience
- Environmentalism
- Illegal immigration
- Making use of medical science (like organ donation)
- Racial discrimination
- Self-defense
- Sexual purity
- Social media use and other media use
- Suicide
- Work ethic

Four Main Questions

- Context: What is the context of this ethical decision?
- Acts: What does the Bible say about this issue, and what creational norms reflect God's design?
- Ends: What sorts of outcomes might various decisions in this situation lead to?
- Agents: What motivations are involved—what virtues are exhibited and what vices are avoided?

9.1 Unethical Killings

Formulate a biblical response to the following scenarios.

SCENARIO ONE

A drunk driver kills a loved one.

_____

_____

_____

_____

SCENARIO TWO

A heated argument between two neighbors turns violent, with one neighbor striking the other in the face with sufficient force to kill him.

_____

_____

_____

_____

SCENARIO THREE

A vicious dog's owners carelessly allow it to run free in the neighborhood until one day the dog attacks and kills a child.

_____

_____

_____

_____

SCENARIO FOUR

After an elderly woman passes away in a nursing home, it is found out that a nurse spent weeks enacting a plan to be written into the woman's will before intentionally administering her a lethal dose of drugs.

_____

_____

_____

9.2 Counsel for Suicide and Euthanasia

Research a biblical counseling resource (book, chapter in a book, booklet, journal or magazine article, blog, sermon, or other media) on suicide and/or euthanasia. Focus on the advice the resource provides on how to respond to someone who has experienced the loss of a loved one to suicide or euthanasia. Suggested resources can be found at biblical counseling websites like CCEF (Christian Counseling and Educational Foundation) or ACBC (Association of Certified Biblical Counselors).

Write a sample dialog of how you would respond to a friend who has experienced such a loss based on the advice you gleaned.

_____

_____

_____

_____

_____

_____

_____

_____

_____

_____

_____

_____

_____

_____

_____

_____

_____

_____

_____

_____

_____

_____

9.3 About Abortion

Work with a classmate to create a helpful pamphlet you can share with friends. Create an inviting design that answers common questions and discusses scriptural concerns. Select from the questions below or create one for the group.

How do you begin a conversation with someone who may intend to have an abortion?

How do you relate the gospel to someone's practical struggles that have led them to consider or to go through with an abortion?

How can I talk to a friend who is considering or who has already had an abortion?

What should I do if a friend is going to secretly get an abortion?

How can you show compassion without compromising the truth when talking with someone being pressured to get an abortion?

How do you persuade and help someone keep the baby, even when difficult circumstances and others' recommendations suggest otherwise?

You will find that people hold various positions on capital punishment. Not everyone you encounter will be equally knowledgeable about why they believe what they believe. How can you best respond to those who have an incorrect view about the justice of the death penalty?

Answer the questions to develop your understanding of the biblically warranted legitimacy of capital punishment.

1. Why does Jesus' teaching about "turning the other cheek" not invalidate the death penalty in murder cases (Matt. 5:38–39)?

   _____

2. If God doesn't get any pleasure from the death of the wicked (Eze. 33:11), how could He have also mandated the death penalty (Gen. 9:5–6)?

   _____

   _____

   _____

   _____

3. If God and the family of the murder victim forgive a repentant murderer, would it be just for the recently converted murderer to be spared from the death penalty?

   _____

   _____

   _____

   _____

10.2 Serving in the Military versus Serving in Combat

For many Christians who serve in the military, it is an honor to serve their country in this way. Serving stateside or fulfilling an assignment in a foreign land outside of wartime is very different from personally going to war and serving in combat. The ethical issue of fighting a just war and doing so justly only arises when one actively participates in a war.

Answer the following questions to assess what considerations are necessary if one is called upon to fight in a war.

1. How would you assess the ethical nature of the war you are being called upon to fight in?

   _____

2. One's responsibility before God is greater than one's responsibility to one's job or one's country. How would you approach your responsibilities if the war you are suddenly involved in is unjust?

   _____

   _____

   _____

3. How would you deal with potential pushback from coworkers, friends, or family who criticized your decision to avoid participating in an unjust war?

   _____

   _____

   _____

   _____

Use the following three steps to begin to formulate an ethical approach to re-forming the current immigration policy in the United States.

1. Research the current statistics on immigration (legal and illegal), looking at the costs and benefits of legal immigration as well as current trends surrounding illegal immigration (where it is happening the most and what is driving it). Offer suggestions to reduce illegal immigration. Be sure to look at sources from a variety of perspectives.

2. Research proposed solutions to the problem of illegal immigration. Evaluate whether they are realistic, effective, and moral.

3. Research ways immigrants are shown compassion and generosity. Evaluate these ways in light of the biblical virtues of prudence, righteousness, and compassion. Balance the real needs many immigrants have with the importance of obeying the law.

In groups, or individually, list issues that would require disobedience to civil authority if they were made into laws.

_____

_____

In groups, or individually, read the following scenarios and provide a response that would promote an ethical disobedience of authority. Include the relevant Scriptures that you would use in support of the ethical disobedience.

SCENARIO 1

A Christian joins a small house church, despite living in a country where house churches are considered illegal. During a worship service, the police interrupt the meeting and the Christian is detained. The totalitarian and religiously oppressive government offers him freedom if he forsakes his faith in Christ. If he does not forsake his faith in Christ and the Bible, he will remain imprisoned in harsh conditions for an undetermined amount of time. Why is it ethical for him to refuse to affirm what the government requires of its citizens?

_____

_____

_____

_____

_____

SCENARIO 2

The government passes a law prohibiting any non-homeschool educational entity (public, private, Christian, etc.) from teaching creationism. What should Christian schools do? What should Christian parents do?

_____

_____

_____

_____

_____

Formulate a biblically wise response to the following scenarios using the given Scripture passages:

1. A friend uses a racial slur in your presence (Ps. 109:2–3; Prov. 10:18).

_____

_____

_____

_____

2. A family member is dismissive about the enduring impact of slavery in America (Job 30:25; Rom. 12:15–16).

_____

_____

_____

_____

_____

3. A teacher discusses the issue of voter identification, and a student in your class asserts that voter identification laws are motivated by racism (Prov. 18:13).

_____

_____

_____

_____

_____

4. A guest preacher is invited to speak to your majority white congregation to promote racial harmony. His message centers on calling the white church members to repent of their "white privilege" (Eph. 2:13–18).

_____

_____

_____

_____

_____

_____

Consult a resource (journal or magazine article, blog, sermon, or other media) on substance abuse or gambling.

Suggested articles:

"Is Marijuana as Safe as We Think?" by Malcolm Gladwell
"Seven Reasons Not to Play the Lottery" by John Piper
"How Casinos Enable Gambling Addicts" by John Rosengren

Additional resources can be found at websites like the Ethics and Religious Liberty Commission (ERLC).

Write a sample dialog of how you would respond to someone pressuring you to engage in one of these vices based on the advice gleaned from the resources that you consulted. You should think through common objections, questions, or pushback that you could face in such a dialog, and then respond in a biblical manner.

_____

_____

_____

_____

_____

_____

_____

_____

_____

_____

_____

_____

_____

_____

_____

_____

_____

11.3 Ethical Challenges with Social Media

Formulate a biblically wise response to the following scenarios using the given Scripture passages.

1. How might you resist the temptation to compare your life with people on social media? Do you think the lives you see on social media are carefully curated, and how might that change the way you see your life? (2 Cor. 10:12)

_____

_____

_____

_____

_____

2. What would be a compassionate response to someone who has been bullied on social media? (Matt. 10:31)

_____

_____

_____

_____

3. What would be an unbiblical response to a person who posted on Twitter a political view with which you strongly disagree? How might you respond to the post with wisdom? (Titus 3:1–2)

_____

_____

_____

4. How might you make use of social media to be a faithful representative of Jesus Christ? (Prov. 12:17–23)

_____

_____

5. Who could you talk to if you have experienced bullying on social media?

_____

_____

_____

Interview a business owner and/or someone who leads a company and who frequently makes difficult decisions to ensure the success of the business without compromising biblical ethics. Select from the questions below and/or add some of your own.

What ethical qualities do you look for when hiring a new employee?

What has been the most difficult ethical decision you have had to make in your position?

How do you balance maximizing business profits with the biblical warnings against the love of money?

Are you aware of any legal yet unethical business practices that give your competitors an edge in the marketplace, and how have you convinced your company to avoid such practices?

What steps do you take to ensure that you are setting a Christlike example for your employees with respect to your work ethic?

What methods do you use to motivate your employees to perform their jobs, and are there certain methods you avoid because they are not consistent with a biblical ethic?

Record a brief video articulating three things you learned and three personal applications.

To edit the human germline means to permanently alter the way someone exists on a cellular level. This change would affect any descendants that a person might have. Human gene editing is irreversible. Little is known about the effects on the individual or on the individual's descendants.

Read the article "Should we edit the human germline?" by Jon Heggie. Write a biblical response to the author's arguments for and against editing the human germline. Weigh the costs and benefits of each and then reach a conclusion.

Responses to Arguments for Human Germline Editing

Immediacy: _____

_____

_____

Permanence: _____

_____

_____

_____

_____

Regulation: _____

_____

_____

Progress: _____

_____

_____

Certainty: _____

_____

_____

_____

Responses to Arguments against Human Germline Editing

Consent: _____

_____

_____

_____

_____

Uncertainty: _____

_____

_____

_____

Permanence: _____

_____

_____

_____

_____

Eugenics: _____

_____

_____

_____

_____

_____

Social: _____

_____

_____

_____

_____

_____

_____

Adapted from:
Heggie, John. "Should we edit the human germline?" Published December 17, 2018. https://
www.nationalgeographic.com/science/article/partner-content-genom-editing

12.2 Paying for Organ Donations?

While considered an impossibility one hundred years ago, organ transplants are now common practices in hospitals, with thousands of procedures performed each year. In many places in the world, these transplants rely on a donation system, in which the donors freely volunteer their organs for this purpose and expect nothing in return. However, there are those who say individuals or their families should be paid for the organs they supply. The idea is that this kind of scenario is a win-win. However, this proposition raises serious ethical questions.

Answer the questions below to develop a biblical response to the practice of paying people for organ donations.

1. **What is the difference between buying an item from a shopping center and buying someone's organs?**

   _____

   _____

   _____

2. **What does the Bible say about our bodies?**

   _____

   _____

   _____

   _____

   _____

   _____

   _____

3. **What does the Bible say about how we are to treat one another?**

   _____

   _____

   _____

   _____

   _____

4. Why is it offensive and degrading to attempt to buy or sell human organs rather than relying on a system of organ donation?

_____

_____

_____

_____

5. What does considering paying someone to obtain an organ for transplantation communicate about one's trust in a sovereign God?

_____

_____

_____

_____

_____

Creation isn't disposable to be thrown away by its consumers, but creation isn't to be worshiped by its users either.

Create a pamphlet on environmental stewardship from a Christian perspective. Use the following questions to guide your categories and content. A main purpose of this pamphlet is to respond biblically to those who want to abuse creation as well as to those who want to idolize creation.

1. **What does the Bible teach about creation in Romans 8:19–23, 2 Peter 3:13, and Revelation 21:1, 5?**

   _____

   _____

   _____

2. **What is foolish about the actions of those described in Romans 1:23–25?**

   _____

3. **What does creation point to in Psalm 19:1–4? How does this truth protect against any notion of idolizing or worshiping creation?**

   _____

   _____

4. **What should be our responses to God as creator of a beautiful and sustaining world?**

   _____

   _____

5. How should you respond to someone who endorses littering freely, wasting natural resources, and refusing to reuse or repurpose usable items?

_____

_____

_____

_____

_____

_____

6. How should you respond to someone who elevates caring for the planet to a level that is on par with idolizing it?

_____

_____

_____

_____

_____

_____

Answer the questions below.

1. What would be an unbiblical, judgmental response to someone going through a divorce? What would be the better response?

   _____

   _____

   _____

   _____

2. What would be an inappropriate response—even if what you say is biblical—if your relationship is not a position of authority or closeness to that person? What would be the appropriate response to someone you are not close to?

   _____

   _____

3. What would be an appropriate, compassionate response to innocent people directly affected by the decisions of others?

   _____

   _____

4. How could distancing yourself from people involved in a divorce or keeping silent about a divorce be unbiblical and hurtful?

   _____

5. Who should you go to for counsel on how to respond biblically to friends or family going through a divorce?

   _____

   _____

Identify what verses in Proverbs 7 teach each of these principles.

_____ **1.** Don't naïvely think you are above sin and its consequences. Stay on guard.

_____ **2.** Don't put yourself in compromising situations.

_____ **3.** Don't approve of or practice immodesty; both men and women can be culpable of either enticing or lusting due to immodest conduct or something immodestly worn.

_____ **4.** Don't approve of or practice dirty or impure communication, be it veiled or obvious.

_____ **5.** Don't play around with physical intimacy that draws you into sinful physical intimacy.

_____ **6.** Don't be duped by flattery and enticement to sin.

_____ **7.** Don't be alone without accountability with someone you might be tempted into sexual sin with; welcome the oversight of others who will help protect you.

_____ **8.** Count the ruinous cost of immorality.

For four of the principles above, provide a specific scenario from your life where it would apply. For each scenario, describe a biblical response, identify how the scenario could lead to ethical compromise, and describe how to biblically seek forgiveness after compromising.

How would you respond to the following scenarios? Be sure to include one or two Scripture passages in your response.

SCENARIO 1

A friend confides in you that she has been struggling with same-sex attraction. She is convinced that it would be wrong to embrace homosexual behavior, but the feelings are just who she is. So, she has decided to embrace both her identity as a lesbian and her identity as a Christian.

SCENARIO 2

A friend reveals to you that he has been reading articles from Christians who argue that the Bible doesn't condemn committed homosexual relationships. He explains how freeing it is to know these desires are natural and have been part of him since childhood, especially since he has been burdened with overwhelming feelings of guilt. Now your friend is convinced that what he feels is natural, normal, and good, and that it does not violate the Bible.

SCENARIO 3

A family member comes out as lesbian and rejects the biblical Christianity that she grew up in. She is not hateful toward you and your family regarding your Christianity, and she still wants to be involved in family activities.

SCENARIO 4

A family member comes out as gay and rejects the biblical Christianity that he grew up in. He is hateful toward you and your family regarding your Christianity, and he wants nothing to do with your family and its get-togethers.

SCENARIO 5

You're excited to start your first job. Part of your training involves watching videos on diversity, including diverse sexual identities, and signing your commitment to embrace such diversity in the workplace.

SCENARIO 6

It's your first opportunity to vote in a national election. Both presidential candidates have records of supporting homosexuality and transgenderism, and both promise further support as president (even though the party of one has historically not supported LGBTQ+ causes).

SCENARIO 7

It's Pride Month, and many social media accounts are posting rainbow symbols to celebrate. Someone at work accuses you of homophobia unless you symbolize your support.

Select a number of factors from Section 13.4 in your textbook that could be involved when a couple is struggling to have children. List the ways that you could offer counsel in this situation, then create a short and simple video of the counsel you would offer to your future self, your future spouse, or a loved one. You may use your list to create a script if it would be helpful.

prayer journal

Prayer Journal 1.1

Read Exodus 34:6. Pray through each of God's attributes mentioned in this verse. Thank God for His mercy, grace, patience, love, and faithfulness. Tell the Lord specific ways each of these attributes have impacted you and why you are grateful for His faultless character and sovereign provision.

Prayer Journal 1.2

Read Genesis 1:31 and Proverbs 3:19–20. Pray that God would show you how to appreciate the good ways He has arranged and organized His universe. Pray that He would open your eyes to the creational norms underlying all aspects of life, even in the broken state the Fall has left the world in. Pray that God would give you grace to embrace and pursue God's good purposes for His creation, even though you might suffer pushback or persecution.

Prayer Journal 1.3

Read Genesis 1:26–30. Pray that God will give you a renewed sense of the dignity and value that each person (man and woman; young and old; rich and poor; any ethnicity) has as an image-bearer of God. Pray that God would give you grace to fulfill the Creation Mandate and that you would be a faithful steward who gives Him glory in all your endeavors.

Prayer Journal 2.1

Read Proverbs 2:6, Job 28:28, and James 1:5. After recognizing the great effects of the Fall on the created order and on the human nature, you should be driven to your knees in dependence on God's grace to help you grapple with the ethical difficulties and the ethical choices that you're faced with in this life. If you seek wisdom from the Lord, He will guide you to rightly apply His Word to your life. Write out a prayer that reflects your heart's desires in relation to the truths found in these verses (and their contexts if need be).

Prayer Journal 2.2

Read Psalm 119:104, 128 and Colossians 2:8. False ways can seem very appealing, yet they are deceptive. Therefore, they should be despised and turned from.Write out a prayer that reflects your heart's desires in relation to the truths found in these verses.

Prayer Journal 2.3

Read 2 Peter 1:3 and Psalm 25:4; 119:15, 48. God's Word provides the sufficient guidance we need to make judgments as we seek to wisely evaluate all things. We need to know His precepts above all else.Write out a prayer that reflects your heart's desires in relation to the truths found in these verses.

Prayer Journal 3.1

Read Ezekiel 36:27. Begin with thanking God for fulfilling His New Covenant promise of the Spirit. Ask for the Spirit's help in recognizing areas of your life that need to be brought into alignment with God's law. Pray for grace to walk in God's statutes. Thank Him for hearing your prayer for Christ's sake. Then step out in faith, believing that God will cause you to walk in His statues as He promised.

Prayer Journal 3.2

Read Proverbs 9:10. Begin with praising God for His infinite wisdom and for being the source of all true wisdom. Confess ways that you have chosen the wisdom of the world over the wisdom of God. Since wisdom begins with a proper recognition of who God is, pray for a greater awareness of God's awesome greatness and power over all creation. Ask for wisdom to make choices in keeping with creational norms for God's glory.

Prayer Journal 3.3

Read Deuteronomy 28:47–48. Pray for grace to recognize how serious joyless service is to God. Ask God for eyes to see the connection between serving God with joy and glorifying God in your service. Confess those times that you have served Him without gladness and ask Christ for forgiveness. Pray that God would satisfy your heart with Himself so that you might serve Him with gladness. Thank Him for His willingness to help you grow in this area as one of His redeemed children.

Prayer Journal 4.1

Read Philippians 4:8. Pray that the inputs into your life would be characterized by all that is listed in this verse. If you have been partaking in a regular diet of things that do not match what is described here, then pray that you would rely on the Holy Spirit to fight the sin in your life and put it off. Pray that you would replace it with that which is excellent or virtuous.

Prayer Journal 4.2

Read Proverbs 4:20–27. Pray that you would be diligent to guard your heart. Everything else in your life flows out from what's in your heart. Pray that you would rightly ponder your path so that you would be established in the right way. Pray that you would remain on the right path rather than swerving into evil.

Prayer Journal 5.1

Read Hebrews 11:6. Begin with praising God for the joy of approaching Him through faith in Christ. Confess ways that doubting God and His Word has negatively impacted your ethical choices. Ask for grace to trust God's Word when the world's lies are pulling you in the opposite direction. Pray for help to make choices that please God, even when those choices look foolish to the world. Thank God for giving you courage to live by faith in a doubting world.

Prayer Journal 5.2

Read 1 John 3:18. Begin with thanking God for His love, especially for demonstrating His love in the gift of His Son. Admit your dependency on God for the ability to love Him and to love others. Pray for help to lovingly apply God's law and creational norms in the various relationships that you have. Ask for wisdom to discern ways that the world abuses love and pray that you would remain faithful to God's definition of love.

Prayer Journal 5.3

Read Romans 15:13. Begin with praising God for being the God of Hope. Bring to God any fears and discouragements you may be experiencing, knowing there is no shame for those who are in Christ Jesus as they approach their Father above. Ask God to fill you with joy and peace through belief in His promises. Pray for help to keep your hope grounded in God's character and promises, and not in the changing circumstances of this life.

Prayer Journal 6.1

Read Psalm 71:19 and 2 Thessalonians 1:11. Thank God for His perfect righteousness and abundant goodness. Realize that praising God for His righteousness means submitting to Him as the Judge of your own sinfulness. Praise God for His goodness in sending Christ to redeem sinful humanity.

Prayer Journal 6.2

Read Proverbs 4:5–11. Pray that the Lord would give you wisdom and understanding through Scripture, godly influences, and His faithfulness in your experiences. He will help you know what to do and when to do it. Ask the Lord for prudence during challenging times and hard decisions. God's wisdom and the understanding He gives are key to practicing the virtue of prudence.

Prayer Journal 6.3

Read Ephesians 6:10–11, 13, Philippians 3:13–14, and Colossians 3:23. Pray that God would give you the strength to be diligent, the patience to stay faithful, and the boldness to be courageous in every aspect of your life. All three virtues are necessary and cannot be pursued one at a time. Ask God to prepare you for scenarios in your life where you will need to use each of these virtues.

Prayer Journal 6.4

Read 1 Corinthians 9:25–27 and 2 Thessalonians 2:4. Pray that God would show you areas of your life where you lack self-control. Pray that God would give you the diligence to pursue temperance in your character. Ask God to give you patience in the big things and in the little things of life.

Prayer Journal 7.1

Read Matthew 12:18–21. Pray that God would conform you into Christ's image by showing you how to imitate His humility, meekness, and gentleness. Pray that God would open your eyes to your own pride, anger, and harshness. Ask for the Spirit to guide you toward humility where you have been proud, meekness where you have often displayed anger, and gentleness where you have been harsh.

Prayer Journal 7.2

Read Romans 2:4. God's kindness and compassion to sinners undeserving of grace or mercy is the main motivator for you to show kindness and compassion to others. You don't have to be a "nice person" to practice kindness and compassion. Pray for a heart that expresses these virtues when you interact with all people, especially those who have needs you can meet.

Prayer Journal 7.3

Read Philippians 4:4–7. Pray that the Lord will help you grow in gratitude, joy, and peace. Ask Him to rid you of anxiety as you seek to rejoice in God's sovereignty over your life. Thank God for the peace He gives that allows you to have a closer and sweeter communion with your Savior. Pray that God will use your practice of these virtues to have an impact on your friends and family as they interact with you.

Prayer Journal 7.4

Read Hebrews 6:17–18. Pray that God would open your eyes to see the areas of your life where small, white, or well-meaning lies have become commonplace. One of the many reasons God is a refuge is because He is trustworthy—He won't and He can't lie. God's faithfulness to being truthful indicates the importance of truth telling. Ask God to help you continually realize that lying and falsehood are products of the Devil's doing.

Prayer Journal 8.1

Read Ephesians 5:10. Make this passage (and its context) a key prayer for your life throughout the year as you seek to make ethical applications in all of life. Write out three specific areas that you would like the Lord to help you to rightly discern how to make ethical decisions.

Prayer Journal 8.2

Read 2 Peter 1:3. You can be confident that God has equipped you and provided for you all that you need to make ethical decisions. It comes through a knowledge of Him. Pray that you would pursue glory and virtue by a dedicated pursuit of a knowledge of God and His Word.

Prayer Journal 9.1

Read Psalm 104:29–30. God is sovereign over life and death—even when a tragedy occurs due to the unethical behavior of others. Therefore, even in the face of tragedy, we can rest under the sovereign plan of God in our lives. That does not remove the sorrow from that tragedy, and it does not justify wrongdoing; the wrongdoing most assuredly will be dealt with by God's judgment in due time. We need not question God's goodness or sovereignty. We can turn to the Lord in prayer by submitting to His providence, seeking His comfort, and appealing for His justice as we await the fulfillment of all things. Consider if you or anyone you know has been affected by premature death, then pray for God's solace to be present in that case.

Prayer Journal 9.2

Read Psalm 139:17–18. You can be assured that God is always mindful of every minute detail of your life. This psalm makes it clear that He cares for you and is always there for you. If you find yourself edging toward despair, then you need renewed hope. Biblical hope is a confident expectation in the fulfillment of God's promises. Biblical hope is a confident expectation because it is grounded in a trustworthy, all-powerful person. What has He really promised in this fallen world in life under the sun? But rest assured that He has promised to give you sufficient grace no matter what you face now. He has promised to make all things right in the end. Pray with confidence that you would live in light of this hope.

Prayer Journal 9.3

Read Psalm 127:3–5. This psalm emphasizes that children are a great gift from God. The psalm explains that one of the blessed purposes of children could be to extend the efforts of parents to triumph in their endeavors against the wicked. Children can complete the unfinished work of their parents. Children reside at the center of their parents' happiness. Pray that you would have a biblical attitude toward children as God's blessing to extend your own life's mission rather than viewing children as a nuisance or obstacle to your own self-made dreams.

Prayer Journal 10.1

Read Genesis 9:6. Pray for your local, state, and national leaders and lawmakers. God's Word is clear that capital punishment is just, and a society that follows God's design is blessed by God. Praise God for making you and every human being in His image. Recognize that we have a responsibility to protect each image-bearer of God. Part of how we can do that is to support the death penalty in our states and countries. Pray for your government officials to do just that.

Prayer Journal 10.2

Read Romans 12:18–19. Pray that God will remove any vengeful desires from your heart. You might be vindictive or enjoy getting back at someone, even if it is in some "small" or "harmless" way. Just wars are a measured and appropriate response that isn't vindictive nor a taking of justice into one's own hand, and therefore out of God's hands. God has established war as a means He uses to punish evildoers and defend the innocent. Guard your own heart and motives.

Prayer Journal 10.3

Read Zechariah 7:9–10. Pray that the Lord would give you a heart of kindness and compassion for those in need. Immigrants are often in that category, regardless of their visa status. Pray for your government officials who constantly wrestle with the best approach for handling immigration and its impact on the country.

Prayer Journal 10.4

Read 1 Peter 2:13–14. Pray that the Lord would give you a heart of obedience and submission to your government and its laws. At the same time, ask God to help you see where the government has overstepped its authority and is creating evil laws or mandating evil requirements for its citizens. The government is used by God to punish those who do evil, but God doesn't expect you to obey a government that is requiring you to do evil. Ask God for prudence and courage.

Prayer Journal 11.1

Read Acts 17:26. Begin by praising God for His wisdom in uniting all humanity through a common ancestor in Adam. Acknowledge that all people are equally valuable and worthy of respect because they are in the image of God. If you have any unconfessed sin of racial prejudice or discrimination, ask God for forgiveness (as well as the courage to make amends with the individual, assuming the offense was more than an internal attitude, and that the individual was harmed by your words or actions). Pray for God to give the church wisdom and grace to promote racial harmony in ways that are consistent with the gospel of Jesus Christ.

Prayer Journal 11.2

Read Galatians 5:22–23. Begin by thanking God for the work of the Holy Spirit. Pray that you may grow in the fruit of the Spirit, yielding more and more to His control in your life. Ask for God's help to resist any peer pressure to engage in vices that lead to substance abuse. If you know someone with an addiction, pray for God to replace the addiction with a greater satisfaction in Christ. Pray that God will bring hope to those who are struggling to overcome an addiction.

Prayer Journal 11.3

Read James 3:6–10. Begin by acknowledging to God how unruly the human tongue is, and that it is not right for us to curse people made in His image. Confess any recent misuse of the tongue and turn to Christ for cleansing and renewal. Pray for grace to guard your tongue and for wisdom to speak that which is pleasing to God. Thank God for being patient with you as you grow in the grace and knowledge of Jesus Christ in your communication.

Prayer Journal 11.4

Read 2 Thessalonians 3:10. Begin by asking God to help you view work the way He does. If you view work as a burden, ask for His help to view work as a gift. If you have an entitlement attitude, where you think you should be able to have what you want without working for it, ask God to correct this attitude within you. Pray that God will enable you to use your talents and opportunities to serve others, knowing that it will honor Him and increase your joy in the Lord. Thank God for how He has provided for your physical needs through the employment He has given your parents.

Prayer Journal 12.1

Read Job 1:21 and 12:10. Humbly recognize your place in God's world. Tell Him that you want to submit to His sovereign dealings and plans for your life. The giver of life is also the taker of the same. This recognition doesn't produce fear or anxiety. This truth produces peace and trust in God's good and just ways. Ask God to give you that peace and trust in Him.

Prayer Journal 12.2

Read Matthew 22:39. This commandment is purposefully broad. One of its many applications includes considering and committing to organ donation. Ask God to give you prudence and wisdom and compassion to love others, possibly in this specific way. Pray that God would help you see the value of loving someone at the end of one's life through organ donation.

Prayer Journal 12.3

Read Psalm 104:24, 31. Praise the Lord for His wonderful works in creation. Thank God for His blessing on you as you use what He has made for your survival and enjoyment. Pray that God will teach you to rejoice in His creation as He does. This rejoicing involves caring for creation and demonstrating responsible stewardship.

Prayer Journal 13.1

Read 1 Peter 3:1–7. What character traits do you need to develop to prepare to be a good husband or wife? Pray that the Lord would help you to develop those character traits.

Prayer Journal 13.2

Read Proverbs 1:20–33. What is God's promise if you heed the call of wisdom? Biblical wisdom offers knowledge, wise counsel, and a solemn respect for God and all things He loves. God offers this wisdom to all, but many people instead choose the way of folly—pursuit of their own earthly goals including revelry, pursuit of power and influence, and willful ignorance. This path ultimately leads to destruction and shame. But the way of wisdom is always free to travel, regardless of past mistakes. Pray to the Lord that you would choose the way of wisdom rather than the way of folly.

Prayer Journal 13.3

Read Jude 1. Pray that the Lord would give you a heart to contend for the faith boldly. Have the compassion to pull people out of the fire while keeping yourself unspotted from the world. Pray for the dependence on God required to keep you in the faith.

Prayer Journal 13.4

Read Psalms 127–128. Pray that you would be this kind of blessing to your parents. Pray that you would seek to imprint this mindset on the next generation.

scripture memory

Chapter 1

ROMANS 1:18–20

For the wrath of God is revealed from heaven against all ungodliness and unrighteousness of men, who hold the truth in unrighteousness; Because that which may be known of God is manifest in them; for God hath shewed it unto them. For the invisible things of him from the creation of the world are clearly seen, being understood by the things that are made, even his eternal power and Godhead; so that they are without excuse:

SIGNIFICANCE

God justly punishes evildoers for the sin they commit. This passage reveals that sinful and rebellious humanity suppresses the truth that the creational order displays. Humans have no excuse for sinning against the powerful and divine God by ignoring the creational norms that undergird His world. Believers have the same revelation, but they also have the Scriptures and the Holy Spirit, both of which show and teach God's will for living for Him. May your life align with God's creational norms and biblical revelation for ethical living.

Chapter 2

ROMANS 3:10–12

As it is written, There is none righteous, no, not one: There is none that understandeth, there is none that seeketh after God. They are all gone out of the way, they are together become unprofitable; there is none that doeth good, no, not one.

SIGNIFICANCE

The Bible describes the nature of all human beings. Not even one person could claim self-righteousness. Their sinful depravity affects their understanding (minds). It affects what they seek after (affections). And it causes them to stray from the right path so that they don't do what's good (wills). This condition makes them overall unprofitable (useless or worthless). Such a human condition brings about many ethical difficulties and makes responding to ethical difficulties problematic apart from God's intervening grace.

Chapter 3

COLOSSIANS 3:1–3, 12

If ye then be risen with Christ, seek those things which are above, where Christ sitteth on the right hand of God. Set your affection on things above, not on things on the earth. For ye are dead, and your life is hid with Christ in God. . . .

Put on therefore, as the elect of God, holy and beloved, bowels of mercies, kindness, humbleness of mind, meekness, longsuffering; . . .

SIGNIFICANCE

The Bible sets forth a clear pattern for ethical living that is rooted in the gospel. Colossians 3 begins with the believer's identity in Christ and then proceeds to call him or her to the regular habit of "putting off the old" and "putting on the new." This redemptive strategy for ethical living is unique to Christian ethics. Christians are called to "put on" mercy, kindness, humility, meekness, longsuffering and more. To do this, Christians need constant reminders of who they are in Christ. Many believers tend to forget their identity in Christ and to approach the Christian life with self-willed effort. This only results in discouragement from not being able to measure up. Returning to the biblical pattern is essential. Remember who you are in Christ, then live as one who has been raised with Christ. This approach to ethics follows God's Word and echoes His redemptive power.

Chapter 4

2 PETER 1:3, 5–7

According as his divine power hath given unto us all things that pertain unto life and godliness, through the knowledge of him that hath called us to glory and virtue: . . .

And beside this, giving all diligence, add to your faith virtue; and to virtue knowledge; And to knowledge temperance; and to temperance patience; and to patience godliness; And to godliness brotherly kindness; and to brotherly kindness charity.

SIGNIFICANCE

Every Christian's calling is to live a life characterized by virtue, empowered by the indwelling Holy Spirit. Growing in Christlikeness begins at conversion when a person places faith in Christ. This growth will certainly continue as that person grows in virtue, knowledge, temperance (self-control), patience (perseverance), godliness, brotherly kindness, and charity (love). In fact, 2 Peter 1:9–10 warns that if a professing Christian lacks these characteristics, then that person should check to see whether he or she is truly saved.

Chapter 5

1 CORINTHIANS 13:13

And now abideth faith, hope, charity, these three; but the greatest of these is charity.

SIGNIFICANCE

The Bible gives priority to the virtues of faith, hope, and love because these virtues ensure that all the other virtues remain God-centered. The tendency of many people who study virtues and character building is to treat these things as part of their own self-improvement project. However, the three central virtues guard against this tendency. Faith looks to God for grace and power to grow in all other virtues for the sake of Christ. Hope looks to God's promises for strength to be virtuous in difficult circumstances. Love for people, which includes relating to them in a virtuous manner, depends on an awareness of God's love and loving Him in return. Therefore, to honor God in virtuous living, one must be a believer (faith) who persists in doing good when life is hard (hope) and who is motivated by treasuring God above all (love).

Chapter 6

PHILIPPIANS 4:8

Finally, brethren, whatsoever things are true, whatsoever things are honest, whatsoever things are just, whatsoever things are pure, whatsoever things are lovely, whatsoever things are of good report; if there be any virtue, and if there be any praise, think on these things.

SIGNIFICANCE

Much of ethical decision making—employing virtue developed in believers by the Spirit—has to do with right thinking. Filling one's minds with biblical, moral, and ethical topics and images goes a long way toward making ethical choices that honor the Lord. Christians should be able to identify sinful patterns and topics and, subsequently, stay away from them. Christians are called to prioritize virtue, as well as righteous and good things, to aid their devotion to God and love for others.

Chapter 7

GALATIANS 5:22–23

But the fruit of the Spirit is love, joy, peace, long-suffering, gentleness, goodness, faith, meekness, temperance: against such there is no law.

SIGNIFICANCE

The list of virtues that believers must develop and practice isn't limited to the list in this passage. But this fruit of the Spirit isn't a buffet where you get to pick and choose which ones you want to emphasize in your life. All Christians are called to practice the fruit of the Spirit—all the virtues in this passage and all the virtues found elsewhere in Scripture. Thankfully, believers can always ask the Spirit to help develop this fruit of virtue in their lives. You might, however, get input from those who know you well and concentrate your efforts for a while on a virtue that you lack altogether or hardly ever practice.

Chapter 8

PSALM 119:97, 101–4

O how love I thy law! it is my meditation all the day. . . .

I have refrained my feet from every evil way, that I might keep thy word.

I have not departed from thy judgments: for thou hast taught me.

How sweet are thy words unto my taste! yea, sweeter than honey to my mouth!

Through thy precepts I get understanding: therefore I hate every false way.

SIGNIFICANCE

This passage highlights the law of God, the psalmist's inward motivation of delight in God's law, and his goal to keep God's Word and to remain aligned with God's judgments. All of this leads him to embrace ethical living, hating every false way. By making God's Word his constant meditation and by submitting himself under God's teachings, the psalmist receives the understanding he needs and the transformed character from within to pursue such an ethical lifestyle.

Chapter 9

MATTHEW 5:21–22

Ye have heard that it was said by them of old time, Thou shalt not kill; and whosoever shall kill shall be in danger of the judgment: But I say unto you, That whosoever is angry with his brother without a cause shall be in danger of the judgment: and whosoever shall say to his brother, Raca, shall be in danger of the council: but whosoever shall say, Thou fool, shall be in danger of hell fire.

SIGNIFICANCE

Jesus expounds upon the original meaning of the law with all its implications. At the root of murder is hatred. The sixth commandment's original intent forbade not only murder but also all that underlies murder as well.

Chapter 10

ROMANS 13:1, 4

Let every soul be subject unto the higher powers. For there is no power but of God: the powers that be are ordained of God. . . .

For he is the minister of God to thee for good. But if thou do that which is evil, be afraid; for he beareth not the sword in vain: for he is the minister of God, a revenger to execute wrath upon him that doeth evil.

SIGNIFICANCE

God has ordained that governments have authority in society. But that authority is for the good and flourishing of individuals, families, and other organizations that make up a society. The authority that governments possess comes from God and they, therefore, are responsible to God for how they uphold and defend the good and oppose and punish the bad.

Chapter 11

MATTHEW 7:12

Therefore all things whatsoever ye would that men should do to you, do ye even so to them: for this is the law and the prophets.

SIGNIFICANCE

The Golden Rule is essential for a society to function in an ethical manner. Without it, the bonds of society are easily broken. Therefore, we should pray that Christ will turn our society toward Him so people will treat others as they wish to be treated.

The beauty of the Golden Rule is the simplicity with which it summarizes the law and the prophets. The Golden Rule applies to all of life. Think of the issues discussed in this chapter. How should you respond to a friend who has experienced discrimination? According to the Golden Rule, you should respond to your friend the same way you would desire your friend to treat you under similar circumstances.

How would you respond if an elected official tried to convince you that a state-sponsored lottery could benefit you? You might think of the lives destroyed by gambling and consider how you would feel if people profited from your misery. Similarly, you probably wouldn't post a cruel comment about an enemy on social media if you reflected on what it would be like to be on the receiving end of a cruel posting. Finally, you probably wouldn't steal what others have worked hard to purchase if you thought of someone doing the same to you.

Chapter 12

And God blessed them, and God said unto them, Be fruitful, and multiply, and replenish the earth, and subdue it: and have dominion over the fish of the sea, and over the fowl of the air, and over every living thing that moveth upon the earth. And God said, Behold, I have given you every herb bearing seed, which is upon the face of all the earth, and every tree, in the which is the fruit of a tree yielding seed; to you it shall be for meat. And to every beast of the earth, and to every fowl of the air, and to every thing that creepeth upon the earth, wherein there is life, I have given every green herb for meat: and it was so.

SIGNIFICANCE

This is the latter half of God's Creation Mandate that He gave to Adam and Eve; it is still in effect today. It outlines a large part of humanity's relationship to the earth and its contents. Subduing the earth and having dominion over it impacts scientific research. Someone's view of humanity and the rest of creation is demonstrated through how that person relates to the world. God blesses people by giving them resources and by providing the responsibility to govern creation. A failure to enjoy and responsibly steward those resources and the knowledge they offer is an affront to God.

Chapter 13

1 THESSALONIANS 4:3–5

For this is the will of God, even your sanctification, that ye should abstain from fornication: That every one of you should know how to possess his vessel in sanctification and honour; Not in the lust of concupiscence, even as the Gentiles which know not God:

SIGNIFICANCE

God's commands make clear God's desired will for His people. One of the keys to fulfilling His will for His people's growth in holy living is to turn away from sexual immorality. Every one of God's people should grow in maturity to take responsible control over their own bodily passions so they behave in ways that are set apart from sin—honorable and above reproach. This will be in stark contrast to the surrounding godless culture, driven by lusts for sexually immoral pleasures.